Exploring the Role of NLP in Overcoming Phobias and Fears

By Rex Morton

Exploring the Role of NLP in Overcoming
Phobias and Fears

Copyright Page

© 2023 by Rex Morton

This book is a work of non-fiction. Unless otherwise noted, the author and the publisher make no explicit guarantees as to the accuracy of the information contained in this book and will not be held responsible for any errors or omissions.

Published by Omniterra Media Inc

First Edition

Visit the author's website at www.rexmorton.com

For information regarding special discounts for bulk purchases, please contact Rex Morton @ Rex@rexmorton.com.

Disclaimer

This book is intended to provide information about the fields of Neuro-Linguistic Programming (NLP) and Cognitive Behavioural Therapy (CBT) and their potential integration. While the author has made every effort to ensure that the information was correct at the time of publication, the author does not assume and hereby disclaims any liability to any party for any loss, damage, or disruption caused by errors or omissions, whether such errors or omissions result from negligence, accident, or any other cause.

The contents of this book should not be used as a substitute for professional advice, diagnosis, or treatment. The reader should always consult with a qualified healthcare provider about any mental health concerns or conditions. Never disregard professional psychological or medical advice or delay in seeking it because of something you have read in this book.

The views expressed in this work are solely those of the author and do not necessarily reflect the views of the publisher, and the publisher hereby disclaims any responsibility for them.

The inclusion of websites, links, or references to other resources does not mean that the author or the publisher endorses the information the organization or website may provide or recommendations it might make. Furthermore, the author does not guarantee the accuracy of the information these resources provide.

The use of any information provided in this book is solely at your own risk.

1.1 A Brief Overview of the Book

Welcome to "Exploring the Role of NLP in Overcoming Phobias and Fears." This book is designed to comprehensively explore the dynamic intersection of Neuro-Linguistic Programming (NLP) and the challenges posed by phobias and fears. We delve into the nature of fears and phobias, their impact on our lives, and traditional methods of dealing with them. The book then leads you to an understanding of NLP, its history, principles, and components. We explore how NLP interacts with our brain functions, explicitly focusing on fear responses. The heart of the book lies in a detailed exposition of various NLP techniques that can be harnessed to overcome phobias and fears, supported by compelling case studies and practical applications. We conclude by envisioning the future of NLP in mental health, highlighting upcoming research and potential breakthroughs.

1.2 The Importance of Understanding Phobias and Fears

Phobias and fears are not mere idiosyncrasies; they are serious conditions that can significantly hamper an individual's quality of life. They can limit one's activities, cause distress, and even lead to other mental health disorders. Understanding phobias and fears is the first step toward dealing with them effectively. This understanding not only aids those suffering from such conditions but also helps their loved ones, therapists, and the broader community to develop empathy and provide appropriate support.

1.3 An Introduction to Neuro-Linguistic Programming (NLP)

NLP, also known as neuro-linguistic programming, is a communication, personal growth, and psychotherapy technique. Developed in the 1970s by Richard Bandler and John Grinder, NLP proposes that there are links between our neurological processes, language, and learned behavioural patterns that can be modified to achieve specific goals in life. In other words, NLP is about understanding "the language of our own mind" and using that understanding to reshape our perceptions and behaviours. It offers a unique and potent toolset that can be applied in various contexts, including the sphere of mental health, specifically in addressing phobias and fears.

In the following chapters, we will unravel the potential of NLP as a tool for overcoming phobias and fears. We will delve deep into the techniques of NLP, explore its practical applications, and hear from those who have successfully used it to conquer their fears. Whether you're a therapist looking for new methods, an individual suffering from phobias, or simply a curious reader, this book aims to provide you with valuable insights into the world of NLP. Let's embark on this journey together.

2.1 Definition and Types of Phobias

Phobias are a type of anxiety disorder characterized by an increasingly irrational fear of specific objects, situations, or activities. They often trigger a strong desire to avoid the feared object or situation, leading to a lot of distress and life interference.

Phobias are generally classified into three primary types:

Specific Phobias are intense, irrational fears of particular objects or situations. Arachnophobia (fear of insects), acrophobia (fear of heights), and claustrophobia (fear of enclosed spaces) are examples of phobias. Specific phobias are the most prevalent form of fear.

Social Phobia (or Social Anxiety Disorder): This involves a fear of social situations, often driven by worries about embarrassment or judgment from others. People with social phobia can fear various social situations, from public speaking to everyday interactions like eating in public.

Agoraphobia: This is a fear of situations where escape might be difficult, or help may not be available if things go wrong. This often includes crowded places, open spaces, or public transportation.

2.2 Common Fears and Their Origins

Fears are basic human emotions triggered by a perceived threat. Unlike phobias, fears tend to be more general and less debilitating. Some common fears include fear of the dark, fear of failure, fear of rejection, and fear of death.

The origins of fears and phobias can be multifaceted. Some are evolutionary, ingrained in our species as survival mechanisms. For example, the fear of snakes or spiders can be traced back to our ancestors who needed to avoid these potentially dangerous creatures. Other fears may originate from personal experiences or traumatic events. For instance, a person might develop a fear of dogs after being bitten by one in childhood.

2.3 The Impact of Phobias and Fears on Daily Life

Phobias and fears can significantly impact an individual's daily life. They can limit one's activities, create distress, and even lead to other mental health disorders such as depression or other anxiety disorders.

For example, a person who fears flying (aviophobia) might avoid jobs or vacations requiring air travel, limiting their career and life experiences. People with social phobia might isolate themselves to avoid social situations, leading to loneliness and depression.

In severe cases, the distress caused by phobias and fears can lead to panic attacks characterized by rapid heartbeat, sweating, trembling, shortness of breath, and a feeling of impending doom.

2.4 Traditional Methods of Treating Phobias and Fears

Traditionally, phobias and fears are treated with a combination of psychotherapy and medications.

Cognitive-Behavioural Therapy (CBT): CBT is a common form of psychotherapy for treating phobias. It involves working with a therapist to identify and change negative thought patterns. Exposure therapy, a type of CBT, involves gradual, repeated exposure to the fear-inducing object or situation until the fear response is diminished.

Medications: While not a cure, certain medications can help manage symptoms of phobias, particularly in combination with therapy. These can include beta-blockers, which can reduce the physical symptoms of anxiety, and selective serotonin reuptake inhibitors (SSRIs), which can help regulate mood.

Relaxation Techniques: Techniques such as deep breathing, meditation, and progressive muscle relaxation can help manage the physiological symptoms of fear and anxiety.

While these traditional methods have proven effective for many, they are not a one-size-fits-all solution.

3.1 The History and Development of NLP

Neuro-Linguistic Programming (NLP) was developed in the 1970s by Richard Bandler, and John Grinder, a linguist, at the University of California, Santa Cruz. Their initial intention was to study the communication methods and behavioural patterns of successful therapists, with a particular focus on the works of family therapist Virginia Satir, hypnotherapist Milton Erickson, and gestalt therapist Fritz Perls.

Bandler and Grinder believed that the skills of these exceptional therapists could be codified and taught to others. This led to the creation of NLP, a set of tools and techniques to facilitate personal development and improve communication and behavioural patterns. NLP has since been adopted in various fields, including education, business, and therapy.

3.2 Basic Principles of NLP

NLP is based on a number of foundational principles:

The Map is Not the Territory: This principle suggests that everyone creates their own subjective experience of reality, or 'map,' which is not the actual 'territory' or objective reality. Personal experiences, beliefs, and perceptions shape these maps.

Experience Has a Structure: NLP proposes that our thoughts, feelings, and behaviours follow patterns and structures that can be recognized and altered. We can change our responses and behaviours by changing the structure of our experience.

If One Person Can Do Something, Anyone Can Learn to Do It: This principle is at the heart of NLP's modeling techniques, which aim to replicate the successful behaviours and strategies of others.

The Meaning of Communication is the Response You Get: According to NLP, effective communication is achieved by what is intended, and the response received. If the response is not as desired, it is up to the communicator to change their approach.

3.3 The Components of NLP: Neurology, Language, Programming

The term "Neuro-Linguistic Programming" reflects its core components:

Neurology: NLP recognizes that our neurology influences our behaviour, the way our brain and nervous system perceive and process experiences.

Language: Language is seen as a vital tool in shaping our thoughts and experiences. It's how we label and interpret our experiences and communicate with others.

Programming refers to the patterns and strategies we use in our thinking and behaviour, often unconsciously. NLP suggests that these 'programs' can be identified and modified to achieve desired outcomes.

3.4 The Benefits and Limitations of NLP

NLP offers several benefits. It provides practical techniques for personal development, improving communication, and changing unhelpful behaviour patterns. It can be used for a wide range of purposes, from enhancing work performance to improving mental health and wellbeing. NLP's emphasis on modeling successful behaviours means it can be tailored to many different contexts and goals.

However, NLP also has its limitations and criticisms. Some critics argue that NLP lacks empirical evidence and rigorous scientific testing. While there are many anecdotal accounts of its effectiveness, more comprehensive research is needed no doubt. But in the end, results matter.

Additionally, the effectiveness of NLP may depend on the skill and expertise of the practitioner. Poorly trained or unethical practitioners could misuse NLP techniques or create unrealistic expectations.

While NLP offers a set of potentially useful tools and techniques for personal development and behaviour change, it should be used with an understanding of its limitations and in conjunction with other evidence-based approaches.

4.1 The Neuroscience of Fear and Phobias

Fear is a primal response hardwired into our brains for survival. It is a part of our body's fight-or-flight response system and is controlled by the amygdala, a small, almond-shaped brain structure responsible for emotional processing. When a threat is perceived, the amygdala is activated, leading to a cascade of physiological responses such as increased heart rate, rapid breathing, and heightened alertness, preparing the body to confront or flee the threat.

Phobias, on the other hand, are a type of anxiety disorder characterized by irrational fear of specific objects, activities, or situations. The neuroscience of phobias is complex and not fully understood, but it is believed that they result from a combination of genetic, environmental, and neurological factors.

Research suggests that people with phobias have an overactive amygdala, which triggers a fear response even when no actual threat is present. This can lead to avoidance behaviours and disrupt daily life. Functional MRI studies have shown that exposure to the feared object or situation can cause increased activity in the amygdala and other brain areas associated with fear processing, such as the insula and the anterior cingulate cortex.

4.2 How NLP Influences Brain Function

Neuro-Linguistic Programming (NLP) operates on the understanding that our thoughts, emotions, and behaviours are actually connected and can be consciously influenced. It proposes that we can change our emotional response to it by changing our internal representations (mental images, sounds, feelings, etc.) of a feared object or situation.

From a neuroscientific perspective, NLP can be seen as a method for rewiring the brain. It encourages new, more positive associations and responses to replace old, fear-inducing ones. For instance, in the case of a phobia, NLP techniques could be used to associate the previously feared object or situation with feelings of relaxation or confidence, thereby reducing the fear response.

NLP also aims to strengthen the connection between the prefrontal cortex, the part of the brain responsible for rational thinking and decision-making, and the amygdala. This can help individuals better regulate their emotional responses and consciously choose how to react to a feared object or situation.

4.3 Neuroplasticity and its Role in Overcoming Fears

Neuroplasticity, or the brain's ability to reorganize itself by forming new neural connections throughout our lives, is a key concept in understanding how NLP can help overcome fears and phobias. This ability of the brain allows us to learn from our experiences and adapt to new situations.

When we repeatedly practice new behaviours or thought patterns, our brain changes in response. Neurons that fire together wire together. Suppose we consistently practice responding to a previously feared object or situation in a new, more positive way. In that case, our brain will begin to form new neural connections that support this response. Over time, this can lead to a significant reduction in fear and anxiety associated with the phobia.

The principles and techniques of NLP align closely with our current understanding of the neuroscience of fear and the brain's capacity for change through neuroplasticity. Using NLP to alter our internal representations and responses to feared objects or situations, we can leverage the brain's plasticity to overcome phobias and fears. The following chapters will delve deeper into specific NLP techniques and their application in treating phobias and fears.

5.1 Visualization Techniques

Visualization is a powerful NLP technique that involves creating mental images to achieve specific outcomes. It is based on the premise that our mind and body often cannot distinguish between real and imagined events. By visualizing a positive experience or outcome, we can condition our mind and body to react as though the positive experience has occurred.

In the context of phobias, visualization can be used to imagine successfully facing a feared object or situation without experiencing fear. For example, if someone fears flying, they might visualize boarding a plane calmly, taking their seat, feeling the plane take off, and experiencing the flight smoothly and without fear. By repeatedly practicing this visualization, they can condition their mind to associate flying with calmness and control instead of fear.

5.2 Anchoring Techniques

Anchoring is an NLP technique that involves associating a specific physical stimulus (the "anchor") with a desired emotional state. Once established, the anchor can quickly and reliably trigger that emotional state.

For instance, a person with a fear of public speaking might establish an anchor (such as pressing their thumb and forefinger together) associated with calmness and confidence. Before they start speaking, they can trigger the anchor to help manage their fear and speak more effectively.

5.3 Reframing Techniques

Reframing is an NLP technique that involves changing how we perceive an event or experience to change our emotional response. In the context of phobias, reframing can help change the perception of the feared object from something threatening to something non-threatening.

For example, someone with a fear of spiders might reframe their perception of spiders by focusing on their role in nature's ecosystem and their relatively harmless nature (most species are not dangerous to humans). This can help reduce the fear and anxiety associated with spiders.

5.4 Swish Pattern Technique

The Swish Pattern is an NLP technique that replaces an unwanted state or behaviour with a desired one. It's called the "Swish" pattern because the change is often swift and dramatic, like the swishing sound.

For instance, someone with a fear of heights might visualize the feeling of dread they get when they look down from a high place (the unwanted state). They then visualize a desired state (e.g., feeling calm and secure). The visualization of the undesirable state is then quickly 'swished' away and replaced with the visualization of the desired state. This technique can help condition the mind to replace the feelings of fear with feelings of calmness and security when facing high places.

5.5 Timeline Therapy

Timeline Therapy is an NLP technique that involves working with the unconscious mind to release negative emotions and limiting beliefs associated with past events. It's based on the idea that our unconscious mind linearly organizes memories, like a timeline.

For example, a person with a fear of dogs due to a traumatic event might use Timeline Therapy to revisit the event in their mind while maintaining a dissociated, third-person perspective. This can allow them to release the fear associated with the memory without reliving the trauma. They might also reframe the event, see it from different perspectives, or imagine a different outcome, which can help change their emotional response to dogs in the present.

These NLP techniques provide powerful tools for overcoming phobias and fears. By applying these techniques, individuals can learn to manage their fears, change their emotional responses, and improve their quality of life.

6.1. How to Apply NLP Techniques in Daily Life

Neuro-Linguistic Programming (NLP) is a set of techniques, principles, and attitudes that can be utilized in various aspects of daily life to improve interpersonal communication, personal development, and achieve specific goals.

A. Setting Goals with the SMART Model

There is a method for setting clear and achievable goals, known as the SMART model. This acronym stands for Specific, Measurable, Achievable, Relevant, and Time-bound.

Specific: Define what you want to achieve in clear and specific terms.

Measurable: Determine how you will measure progress toward your goal.

Achievable: Make sure your goal is within your capability and resources.

Relevant: Ensure your goal aligns with your overall values and long-term objectives.

Time-bound: Set a deadline to keep you focused and motivated.

For example, instead of a vague goal like "I want to lose weight," a SMART goal would be "I want to lose 10 pounds in the next three months by exercising four times a week and reducing my sugar intake."

B. Building Rapport

Building rapport is a crucial part of NLP, and it can be applied in everyday interactions to improve communication. Matching and mirroring body language, speech patterns, and even breathing can create a sense of familiarity and understanding. For example, subtly matching the posture or gestures of the person you're talking to can help establish a connection and facilitate smoother communication.

C. Positive Affirmations and Visualization

NLP techniques also involve using positive affirmations and visualization to shape behaviour and attitudes. By visualizing a desired outcome and speaking to yourself in positive terms, you can work towards achieving your goals. For instance, if you're nervous about a presentation, visualize yourself delivering it successfully and affirm to yourself that you're capable and prepared.

6.2. Professional Applications of NLP in Therapy

NLP has found applications in various professional fields, especially in therapy, where it is used to help individuals overcome fears, phobias, and limiting beliefs.

A. Overcoming Phobias

NLP techniques can be used to help individuals overcome phobias. For instance, the 'Fast Phobia Cure' technique involves having the client visualize their fear from a dissociated, third-person perspective and then altering the visualized experience to make it less frightening. This can help to 'reprogram' the emotional response to the fear stimulus.

B. Enhancing Communication in Therapeutic Settings

NLP can also enhance communication between therapists and their clients. By utilizing techniques like the Meta-Model – a set of questions designed to clarify and explore more profound layers of personal experience – therapists can help clients uncover hidden beliefs or assumptions that may be causing distress.

C. Modifying Unhelpful Behaviours

The 'Swish' technique in NLP replaces an unhelpful behaviour or response with a more beneficial one. This technique involves visualizing the unwanted behaviour, then 'swishing' it away and replacing it with the desired behaviour. For instance, a person might use the Swish technique to curb the urge to smoke by replacing the thought of a cigarette with an image of themselves being healthy and active.

6.3. Precautions and Ethical Considerations

While NLP offers a variety of powerful tools for personal development and therapy, it's essential to be aware of ethical considerations and precautions.

A. Respect for Autonomy

NLP practitioners should respect the autonomy and individuality of each person. Techniques should not be used to manipulate or control others against their will. The goal of NLP should always be to facilitate growth, development, and positive change that aligns with the individual's values and desires.

B. Confidentiality

Especially in therapeutic settings, confidentiality is a fundamental ethical principle. Information shared during therapy sessions should not be disclosed without the individual's consent, except in cases where there is a risk of harm to the individual or others.

C. Competence and Training

NLP techniques should only be applied by those with appropriate training and competence. Misapplication of NLP techniques can lead to ineffective outcomes or even harm. Therefore, anyone wishing to practice NLP professionally should undergo thorough training and certification.

D. Avoiding Over-Promise of Results

NLP practitioners should avoid making unrealistic promises or guarantees about the results of NLP techniques. While NLP can be a powerful tool for change, its effectiveness can vary depending on the individual and the context.

E. Informed Consent

Before beginning any NLP intervention, practitioners should ensure that the individual has given informed consent. This means they have been provided with clear, comprehensive information about the nature and purpose of the **intervention,** any potential risks, and their right to decline or withdraw at any time.

NLP is a versatile and powerful tool that can be applied in various aspects of daily life and in professional settings, including therapy. However, its use should always be guided by respect for the individual's autonomy, confidentiality, and informed consent and should only be carried out by appropriately trained and competent practitioners.

7.1. The Future of NLP in Mental Health

As we gain a deeper understanding of the human mind and its intricacies, the future of Neuro-Linguistic Programming (NLP) in mental health looks promising. NLP has already shown potential in various areas of mental health, such as anxiety disorders, phobias, and post-traumatic stress disorder (PTSD). Its focus on empowering individuals to understand and alter their thought processes aligns well with the trend toward more patient-centered care in mental health.

A. Personalized Therapy

One potential future direction is the increasing use of NLP in personalized therapy. By using NLP techniques, therapists can tailor their approach to the individual's unique thought patterns and experiences, leading to more effective and customized treatment plans.

B. Group Therapy

NLP may also find broader application in group therapy settings. By teaching group members to understand and communicate more effectively with one another, NLP could help facilitate more profound and meaningful group interactions, enhancing the therapeutic outcomes of group therapy.

7.2. Technological Advancements and Their Role in NLP

The advent of technology has brought about new possibilities for applying NLP. From virtual reality to artificial intelligence, technological advancements are poised to shape the future of NLP.

A. Virtual Reality and Augmented Reality

Virtual Reality (VR) and Augmented Reality (AR) technologies offer exciting possibilities for NLP. For instance, VR could be used to create immersive experiences that help individuals confront and overcome their fears in a safe and controlled environment, enhancing the effectiveness of NLP techniques like the Fast Phobia Cure. Similarly, AR could be used to overlay helpful NLP cues or reminders in the individual's real-world environment, supporting the application of NLP techniques in daily life.

B. Artificial Intelligence

Artificial intelligence (AI) could also play a role in the future of NLP. Machine learning algorithms could be used to analyze and understand an individual's linguistic patterns more deeply, providing insights that could enhance the application of NLP techniques. AI could also be used to deliver personalized NLP interventions, adapting in real-time to the individual's responses.

7.3. Ongoing Research and Potential Breakthroughs

While NLP has been around for several decades, there is still much to be learned, and ongoing research continues to explore its potential.

A. Evidence-Based Research

More rigorous, evidence-based research on the efficacy of NLP is needed. Such research would also help to refine NLP techniques and identify the conditions for which they are most effective.

B. Integration with Other Therapies

Another promising area of research is the integration of NLP with other therapeutic approaches. For instance, NLP techniques could be combined with cognitive-behavioural therapy or mindfulness-based therapies to create more comprehensive and effective treatment protocols.

C. Understanding the Neurological Basis of NLP

Lastly, neuroscience could play a crucial role in future NLP research. By exploring how NLP techniques influence brain function and structure, we could gain a deeper understanding of why these techniques work and how to optimize them.

In conclusion, the future of NLP looks bright, with promising potential applications in mental health, exciting possibilities brought about by technological advancements, and ongoing research paving the way for new breakthroughs. As we continue exploring this fascinating field, we can look forward to new insights and tools to help us better understand and shape our minds.

Rex Morton is a renowned author and researcher in the United Kingdom with a passionate interest in the human mind, specifically in Cognitive Behavioural Therapy (CBT) and Neuro-Linguistic Programming (NLP).

Morton has spent a considerable portion of his professional life diving deep into the theories and principles that form the backbone of these two compelling fields. His fascination with NLP led him to complete an extensive certification program, solidifying his understanding of this innovative approach to understanding human behaviour.

Although Morton does not have clinical experience, his intense curiosity and dedication to studying these subjects have made him a respected figure in the field. He has thoroughly researched the integration of NLP techniques into CBT, offering fresh perspectives and insights into how these two methodologies can complement each other to enhance understanding of human cognition and behaviour.

As an author, Morton has successfully communicated his knowledge and passion to a broader audience, making complex psychological theories accessible to professionals and interested laypersons. His writing is characterized by a clear, engaging style and a focus on the practical application of theories, making them relevant to everyday life.

In his personal life, Morton is an ardent lover of the natural world, often spending his free time exploring the British countryside. His passion for landscape photography allows him to capture and share the beauty of these excursions. Despite his accomplishments, Morton is known for his humility and eagerness to continue learning. His work continues to inspire those interested in the intricate workings of the human mind and the exciting possibilities presented by the integration of NLP and CBT.

If you've found the content of this book enlightening and wish to continue your journey of understanding the human mind, I warmly invite you to visit my website at www.rexmorton.com. The website serves as a hub of knowledge where I share my latest findings, thoughts, and insights on the integration of NLP and CBT.

I also encourage you to subscribe to the newsletter available on the website. By subscribing, you'll receive regular updates on a range of topics, from detailed discussions on specific NLP techniques and their application in CBT, to the latest research in the field.

The newsletter is also the first place I'll share news of upcoming releases. Whether it's the announcement of a new book, the launch of an online course, newsletter subscribers will be the first to know. This is a great opportunity to continue learning directly from me, deepening your understanding of NLP and CBT, and enhancing your skills in applying these techniques in your own life or professional practice.

I'm looking forward to sharing this journey with you.